# OUR
# EXTREME
# EARTH

## ACKNOWLEDGMENTS

Design and picture research by Dynamo Limited

Author: Anne Rooney
Publishing Director: Piers Pickard
Publisher: Hanna Otero
Art Director: Ryan Thomann
Commissioning Editor: Catharine Robertson
Print Production: Lisa Taylor

Published in July 2020 by Lonely Planet Global Ltd

CRN: 554153
ISBN: 978 1 83869 085 4
www.lonelyplanetkids.com
© Lonely Planet 2020

Printed in Singapore
2  4  6  8  10  9  7  5  3  1

All rights reserved. No part of this publication may be reproduced, stored in a retrieval system or transmitted in any form by any means, electronic, mechanical, photocopying, recording or otherwise except brief extracts for the purpose of review, without the written permission of the publisher. Lonely Planet and the Lonely Planet logo are trademarks of Lonely Planet and are registered in the US Patent and Trademark Office and in other countries.

Although the author and Lonely Planet have taken all reasonable care in preparing this book, we make no warranty about the accuracy or completeness of its content and, to the maximum extent permitted, disclaim all liability from its use.

## STAY IN TOUCH
lonelyplanet.com/contact

Lonely Planet Offices

### AUSTRALIA
The Malt Store, Level 3, 551
Swanston St., Carlton, Victoria 3053
T: 03 8379 8000

### UK
240 Blackfriars Rd.,
London SE1 8NW
T: 020 3771 5100

### IRELAND
Digital Depot, Roe Lane
(off Thomas St.), Digital Hub,
Dublin 8, D08 TCV4

### USA
155 Filbert St., Suite 208
Oakland, CA 94607
T: 510 250 6400

MIX
Paper from
responsible sources
FSC™ C021741

Paper in this book is certified against the
Forest Stewardship Council™ standards.
FSC™ promotes environmentally responsible,
socially beneficial and economically viable
management of the world's forests.

Lonely planet Kids

# OUR
# EXTREME
# EARTH

Anne
Rooney

3 1150 01761 6729

## Explore amazing habitats
## around the world

BOISE PUBLIC LIBRARY

# CONTENTS

# WELCOME TO OUR EXTREME EARTH

Our world is one of extremes: from the hottest and driest deserts to the coldest ice fields, from the most desolate wilderness to forests teeming with life. It is a planet of contrasts and beauty, of challenge and plenty. In this book, you will discover some of the most amazing and wild places on Earth. You will see deserts, mountains, caves, forests, glaciers, the deep ocean, and raging rivers, and discover how life clings on even in desolate and challenging places.

## OUR CHANGING WORLD

Earth today is the result of billions of years of change. It is changing still, and with climate change, it could change faster than ever before. Some of the landscapes you see here won't last. Others will become yet more extreme.

Our planet has such varied environments because it has a hot, shifting interior and a surface with weather and oceans.

## POWER FROM WITHIN

Beneath Earth's hard outer crust lies a thick layer of scorching, semi-molten rock called magma. Plates of land that make up the continents creep around the planet as the magma slowly moves beneath them. In some places, volcanoes hurl out molten rock, called lava. It hardens as it meets the cool air or water. Around live volcanoes, poisonous gases pour from the hot ground, and scalding pools of acidic, mineral-rich water form. Around old, dead volcanoes, rock has sometimes eroded (been worn away) to leave bizarre spikes, ridges, and towers of hard rock that was once molten inside the volcano.

## WORN AWAY

Earth is made of many different types of rock. Some are very hard and erode only slowly. Others are soft, or dissolve slowly in water. These rocks change shape or even disappear completely over time. Rock can be worn away by running water and by being blasted with sand and water carried on winds.

Wind and rain can also strip away soil. If there is no soil, just sand or bare rock, then little can grow. Areas with no soil are often deserts, where it is also very dry. Where there is soil, plants can take root, and roots help to hold more soil in place. Where it is warm and wet and there is soil, forests teeming with life can grow.

## FROM TOP TO BOTTOM

Earth has different climate zones, meaning that different areas are hotter or colder, wetter or drier. Generally, areas near the poles are coldest, and the hottest regions are near the equator (an imaginary line around the middle of Earth). In between, temperate regions are just right for many types of life, being neither too hot nor too cold.

Climate and landscape work together. Mountains can stop clouds in their tracks, making them drop their water as rain. Land behind the mountains might then be very dry—a desert. But rain makes rushing rivers or freezing glaciers, which can wear passages through mountains over millions of years. Wind and rain can even wear mountains down to flat plains.

## LIVING PLANET

Earth is home to millions of different species (types) of plants, animals, fungi, and microbes adapted to live in all environments, even the most hostile. Where the climate is kind, life can be so abundant that organisms (living things) struggle to find a little space of their own to occupy. They adapt to specialize, helping them compete with others. Where the climate and landscape are harsh, organisms adapt to cope with difficult conditions and lack of food. Some have made some strange changes to their bodies and lives in order to colonize the most challenging places on our extreme Earth.

# AT HOME IN A HABITAT

A habitat is the natural home of an organism, such as a plant or animal. It must provide suitable shelter and a source of food and water. Even some of the most extreme environments on Earth provide habitats where plants and animals can live. The conditions that are important to organisms include temperature, weather, the kind of landscape, and what else lives there —things they can eat, or that might eat them!

Some habitats are very pleasant and easy to live in. These usually attract a lot of organisms. Fewer organisms can survive in harsher environments. Plants and animals often need to adapt special ways of coping to live in extreme conditions.

In this book, each location has a label describing the habitat it offers. For places on land, the first part of the label shows the climate and the second shows the type of environment (the biome).

Water habitats generally only have one label, showing whether it is marine (oceans and seas), freshwater (rivers and lakes), or ice.

 | **TROPICAL / RAINFOREST**

In the example above, the first part shows you this is a hot, humid place; the second tells you that the environment is a forest, full of trees and other plants.

## A PLACE IN THE SUN?

The climate is the long-term pattern of weather. Different climates produce different habitats. For example, tropical forests grow in hot, humid climates.

Some places have comfortable climates, neither very hot nor very cold, not too rainy or too dry. Many kinds of plants and animals can live in these types of environments. Other places have extreme climates. Scorching temperatures, droughts (dry periods), freezing cold, howling winds, and torrential rain are all challenging conditions for organisms.

Scientists often divide climates into five main types:

- **Tropical:** warm and wet all year. The average temperature is at least 64.4°F (18°C) every month. Tropical areas are near the equator, where there is little difference between summer and winter.
- **Arid (or dry):** warm or cold, with little or no rain.
- **Temperate:** neither very hot nor very cold, but with different seasons. The coldest month has an average temperature between 32°F (0°C) and 64.4°F (18°C), and in at least one month the average is over 50°F (10°C).
- **Continental:** the average temperature is below freezing (32°F/0°C) for one month, and above 50°F (10°C) for at least one month.
- **Polar:** cold, with the average temperature always below 50°F (10°C).

## BY LAND AND SEA

As well as different climates, the world has different biomes—"life zones" where plants and animals of different types live. Some biomes, like "forest," are found all over the world and come in various forms. The main biomes are:

- **Forest:** this can be hot, wet, tropical rainforest, woodland found in temperate areas, or boreal forest in cold areas.
- **Desert:** this can be hot or cold, rocky or sandy, but is always dry.
- **Grassland, plains, or scrubland:** these have wide expanses of low-growing plants.
- **Tundra:** this is flat and cold with a layer of ice just below the surface, so not much can grow there.
- **Freshwater:** rivers and lakes.
- **Marine:** oceans.
- **Ice:** polar ice caps, sea ice, and glaciers.

# THE HAWAIIAN ISLANDS

### HAWAII, USA

A string of islands lies stranded in the middle of the Pacific Ocean—one of the most isolated landmasses on Earth. On some, jet-black rock oozes scalding hot lava into the sea, where it hisses and steams.

The eight main islands and 129 minor islands formed from lava erupting over millions of years and piling up on the ocean bed. Many of these volcanic mountains are now dormant. Mauna Kea, the tallest, last erupted 4,600 years ago.

When you think of Hawaii, you probably think of warm, tropical beaches. But between them, the islands actually have four of Earth's five main climate zones, ranging from desert to near-glacial. The summit of Mauna Kea has freezing temperatures, winter snow, and hurricane-force winds.

## LIFE ON THE VOLCANO

Wēkiu bugs live only on the summit of Mauna Kea, where little else can survive. They are a type of seed bug, but here, only seedless moss and lichens grow on the bare, frozen rocks. The bugs have a gruesome way of surviving: they eat the bodies of dead insects blown up the mountainside by the wind. It's a bug-eat-bug world on this frozen volcano. Antifreeze in their blood helps them live in the extreme cold.

**RISING OVER 33,000 FT. (10,000 M) FROM THE SEABED, MAUNA KEA IS ACTUALLY TALLER THAN MOUNT EVEREST! BUT MOST OF IT IS SUBMERGED UNDERWATER, MAKING IT THE TALLEST BUT NOT THE HIGHEST MOUNTAIN IN THE WORLD.**

The Nënë lives only in Hawaii and is the world's rarest goose.

# THE SONORAN DESERT

## SOUTHWESTERN USA & NORTHWESTERN MEXICO

Scorching hot, the Sonoran Desert is far from deserted. It has more varied plant life than any other desert in the world—including weird and wonderful cacti that hoard their water carefully.

Most deserts are extremely dry all year, but the Sonoran has a subtropical climate with up to 15 in. (38 cm) of rain a year, mostly falling in the summer. With the rains, it bursts into life.

The edge of the desert is thornscrub, halfway between desert and tropical forest. It's alive with birds, such as the roadrunner, and desert animals, such as tortoises, Gila monsters, coyotes, and even mountain lions.

### LIFE IN THE DESERT

The creeping devil cactus is the only plant that lives in the extremely dry Magdalena area of the Sonoran. It grows horizontally, seeming to crawl along parallel to the ground as its older parts die and new parts grow. The old parts then rot and put goodness back into the ground, feeding new growth.

**THE SONORAN DESERT IS THE HOTTEST DESERT IN NORTH AMERICA—TEMPERATURES OFTEN REACH 120°F (49°C) IN THE SUMMER.**

**" THIS HUGE DESERT IS THE LARGEST IN NORTH AMERICA, COVERING AROUND 120,000 SQ MILES (310,800 SQ KM). "**

GILA MONSTER

COYOTE

THE WILY ROADRUNNER CAN RUN AT SPEEDS OF 20 MPH (32 KPH), AND EATS VENOMOUS SNAKES!

# THE MENDENHALL GLACIER

**EVERY YEAR, SALMON SWIM AND LEAP UPSTREAM IN HUGE NUMBERS**

## JUNEAU, ALASKA, USA

Ice 100 ft. (30 m) thick creeps down Thunder Mountain to fall into a lake of its own making. Chunks break off and float away as icebergs.

Glaciers are "rivers of ice." They form when snow builds up year after year, collecting faster than it melts. The snow is squashed, getting packed solid. The bottom of the glacier then melts under pressure, creating a slippery layer of water, and the whole glacier flows slowly downhill. The Mendenhall Glacier moves just 24 in. (60 cm) a day.

The glacier (and the huge Juneau Ice Field that feeds it) formed 3,000 years ago but is now melting and rapidly retreating due to climate change. Mendenhall shrunk only 0.5 miles (800 m) between the years 1500 and 1958 but has retreated 2 miles (3.2 km) since 1958.

As the glacier melts, gaping caves open up beneath the ice. These grow larger and larger until finally they collapse, the ice above crashing down.

## LIFE ON THE GLACIER

Nothing lives on the ice itself, but salmon spawn (lay eggs) where streams pour into Mendenhall Lake. Eagles and black bears gather to feast on the fish each spring.

**ICE TAKES 200–250 YEARS TO TRAVEL FROM THE TOP OF THE GLACIER TO THE LAKE.**

If climate change continues at current rates, the glacier will disappear in around 80 years.

**HUGE BALD EAGLES CAN DIVE AT SPEEDS OF 75 MPH (120 KPH) TO SNATCH SALMON FROM THE WATER.**

# ANTELOPE CANYON

## ARIZONA, USA

Unearthly walls of twisted, colored rock make Antelope Canyon bizarre and spectacular. Known as a slot canyon, it has been created by fast-flowing floodwater cascading through cracks in the rock and cutting out a passage.

Flash floods pour huge amounts of water into creeks that gush through the rocks. The water runs fast and furious, eroding the soft sandstone surface. When the flood subsides, hot, dry weather brings sandstorms that polish and smooth the exposed rock, revealing all shades of pink and red.

Over thousands of years, the rocks have eroded into beautiful, twisting shapes. The canyon has two parts: the upper canyon, called the Crack, has steep, deep sides and just a narrow gap at the bottom. The lower canyon, separated from the Crack, is called the Corkscrew and has amazing, swirling shapes carved from the rock.

**THE CANYON STILL FLOODS SUDDENLY, EVEN WHEN IT IS NOT RAINING—RAIN FALLING MILES UPSTREAM OF THE CANYON CAN CAUSE WATER TO RUSH IN.**

### LIFE IN THE CANYONS
The canyons are in Navajo tribal territory and might have been used as a place to hide in the 1860s when US forces tried to drive the Navajo from their land.

The canyons are just 3.3 ft. (1 m) wide in places and up to 165 ft. (50 m) deep.

# MANGROVE FOREST

## CHIAPAS, MEXICO

In the lush world of the mangrove, the tangled roots of the trees make a thickly wooded underwater forest where fish and other animals lurk.

Rivers carry nutrient-rich freshwater into the area, and the tide brings in saltwater from the ocean twice a day. The mix of saltwater and freshwater teems with life: microbes that feed worms and shellfish are in turn eaten by larger fish, birds, and crocodiles. The mangroves provide invaluable shelter and food for many different species.

## LIFE IN THE MANGROVE FOREST

Most plants would die in saltwater, but mangrove trees are cleverly adapted to the seawater that floods the swamp. Some have stilt-like roots and some grow roots that stick up out of the ground like straws, helping the tree to get air despite growing in waterlogged soil. The trees leak out excess salt through their leaves.

**PELICANS, EGRETS (BELOW), AND OTHER WATERBIRDS PREY ON THE MANY FISH.**

**" MANGROVE FORESTS ARE PERMANENTLY FLOODED WITH BOTH SALTWATER AND FRESHWATER—THE WATER HAS A HIGH SALT CONCENTRATION WHEN THE TIDE COMES IN. "**

Mangroves are an essential ecosystem, but they are at risk of deforestation.

OCELOTS (ABOVE), JAGUARS, AND WILD BOARS (TOP RIGHT) STALK THE DRIER LAND OF THE MANGROVE AND COME TO THE WATER TO DRINK.

# DEATH VALLEY

## CALIFORNIA, USA

**DESERT BIGHORN SHEEP ARE SURPRISINGLY FAST AND CAN CLIMB STEEP, ROCKY MOUNTAINS.**

A bone-dry, boiling hot desert of rock and sand lies within sight of permanent snow on the surrounding mountain peaks. There is no shelter from the burning sun.

The mountains shade the low-lying valley from rain so that in some years none falls at all. As air comes into the valley, any water it is carrying falls as snow on the mountaintops. On the rare occasions it does rain, the valley comes briefly alive with flowers—their seeds having been dormant through years of dry weather.

### LIFE IN THE DESERT

Bighorn sheep can live for several days without drinking and can lose up to a third of their body weight through dehydration. They fill up with gallons of water when they get the chance. Kangaroo rats don't drink at all but get all the fluid they need from the seeds and plants that they eat. Desert tortoises can't control their own temperature and have to hide in burrows for nine months of the year when the weather is at its hottest or coldest.

**" THE HIGHEST AIR TEMPERATURE ON EARTH WAS RECORDED IN DEATH VALLEY: A SWELTERING 134°F (56.7°C)! "**

DEATH VALLEY IS THE LOWEST POINT IN NORTH AMERICA, AT 282 FT. (86 M) BELOW SEA LEVEL.

A KANGAROO RAT'S STRONG BACK LEGS ENABLE IT TO JUMP MORE THAN 6.6 FT. (2 M) IN A SINGLE BOUND!

There is little or no rainfall here: 0-2 in. (0-5 cm) per year!

# SALAR DE UYUNI

## UYUNI, BOLIVIA

Near Potosí in Bolivia, blindingly white salt flats stretch all the way to the horizon. And when rain floods the flats, the water becomes the most reflective surface on Earth, mirroring the sky perfectly to create an unreal landscape.

The land here is absolutely flat and featureless except for the peaks of a few ancient volcanoes that form islands when the flats flood. This astonishing landscape was created when a lake, once 400 ft. (120 m) deep, dried up thousands of years ago, leaving a thick crust of salts. Several feet beneath the surface lies a layer of concentrated saltwater mud.

### LIFE ON THE SALT FLATS

When the rains come, the lake bed floods and the salts dissolve. Flamingos flock to nest here, feeding on saltwater algae that grow in the water. Cacti live on the islands, taking 1,200 years to grow up to 40 ft. (12 m) tall. When the beds are dry, people mine the salt to sell and use as a building material. Even taking 27,500 tons (25,000 tonnes) of salt each year, there is still enough to last 400,000 years!

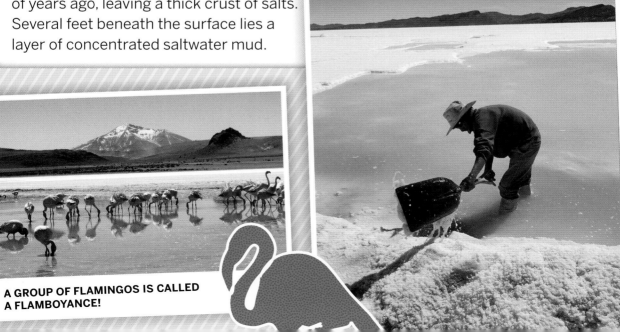

**A GROUP OF FLAMINGOS IS CALLED A FLAMBOYANCE!**

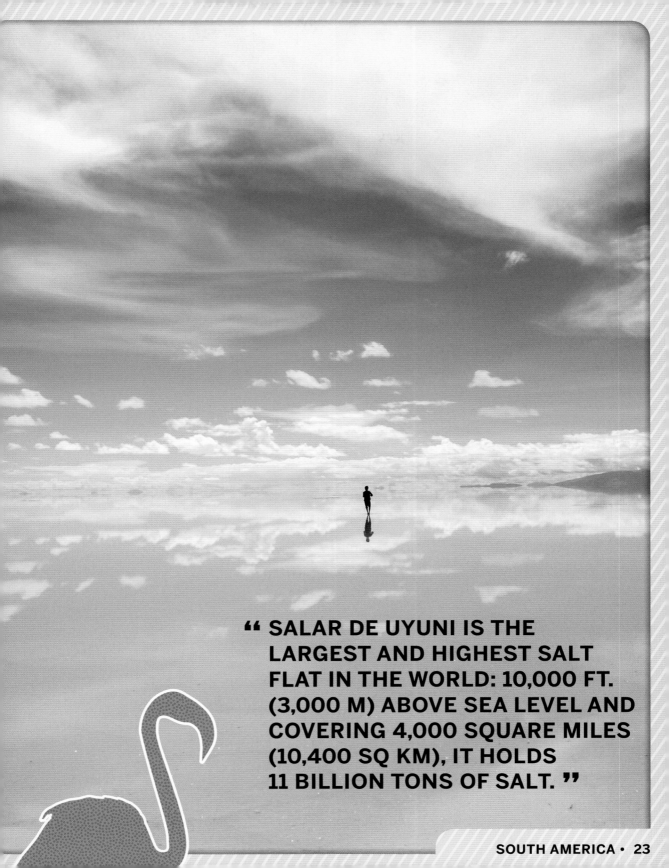

" SALAR DE UYUNI IS THE LARGEST AND HIGHEST SALT FLAT IN THE WORLD: 10,000 FT. (3,000 M) ABOVE SEA LEVEL AND COVERING 4,000 SQUARE MILES (10,400 SQ KM), IT HOLDS 11 BILLION TONS OF SALT. "

# TAPAJÓS-XINGU MOIST FORESTS

## AMAZON BASIN, BRAZIL

Lush tropical forest tangles right down to the edges of rivers teeming with life in the Amazon basin. One of the most complex forests in the world, the Tapajós-Xingu is trapped between three rivers: the Amazon (the largest river in the world), the Tapajós, and the Xingu. Twisting lianas (woody vines) make a unique and dense lower level. Some animal species have lived here for thousands of years and evolved in unique ways. There is so much competition from other plants and animals that the challenge is to find a niche that is not filled already in this crowded ecosystem.

### LIFE IN THE FOREST

Sloths live high in the trees, rarely visiting the ground. They hang upside down from branches, anchored by strong, curved claws and safe from most predators. Hoatzin chicks have claws on their wings so that they, too, can cling to vines and bark. You can also see pumas, tapirs (far right), manatees, caimans, river dolphins, toucans, and macaws living in the forest and rivers.

Local people have farmed the forest sustainably for thousands of years. There are around 80 tribes living in the Amazon area who have never been in contact with other human beings. But the forest is threatened by uncontrolled development, with people cutting down trees for wood and burning forest to clear land for industrial farming and building.

TOUCANS HAVE LARGE COLORFUL BILLS WITH SERRATED EDGES, PERFECT FOR PEELING FRUIT!

> **"IT IS PART OF THE LARGEST RAINFOREST IN THE WORLD, COVERING 2.1 MILLION SQUARE MILES (5.5 MILLION SQ KM)."**

**HOATZINS BUILD THEIR NESTS OVERHANGING THE WATER.**

These forests get up to 6.5 ft. (2 m) of rain a year!

# CAÑO CRISTALES

## (THE LIQUID RAINBOW)

### SIERRA DE LA MACARENA, COLOMBIA

**THE ROCKS ARE 1.7 BILLION YEARS OLD, THE OLDEST IN SOUTH AMERICA.**

A "liquid rainbow" cascades through 330 ft. (100 m) of linked waterfalls and lakes on one of the oldest rock formations on Earth: the Guiana Shield. The brilliant colors are produced by plants that grow on the riverbed, fed by the very high mineral content of the water.

The rocks are also rich in minerals like phosphorous and iron, which stunt plants growing on the land. Plants along the riverbanks grow only about 0.4 in. (1 cm) a year—but they are made up for by the stunning underwater display.

### LIFE IN THE WATER

The plant *Macarenia clavigera* is a riverweed that is green most of the year. But for a few weeks at the end of the dry season (from September to November), it bursts into color, putting on a dazzling display of pink, red, purple, yellow, and green beneath the water. The color varies depending on the temperature, amount of sunlight, and rainfall during the year. The plant grows nowhere else in the world.

" **THIS AREA HOLDS A FIFTH OF ALL THE FRESH SURFACE WATER IN THE WORLD!** "

# MARBLE CATHEDRAL

## PATAGONIA, CHILE

This island made of marble has been sculpted over thousands of years by the waters of a glacial lake. A network of swirling caverns and hanging rocks makes a fantasy landscape, some of it below water.

Water has poured into Lake General Carrera from melting glaciers in the Andes Mountains for more than 10,000 years. Sweeping currents have eaten into the marble, creating glittering caves that reflect the brilliant blue of the water. The appearance of the caves changes with the seasons as the water level rises and falls; the lake is deeper in the summer when it floods with meltwater.

The caves are still forming today. The surface of the rock has tiny holes —like honeycomb—that slowly join to make new hollows and caves. There are other sculpted caves all around the shores of the lake, and a nearby hanging glacier—positioned high in the mountains—pours water down a plunging waterfall into the lake.

GENERAL CARRERA IS CHILE'S LARGEST LAKE AND ONE OF THE DEEPEST IN THE WORLD, AT 1,923 FT. (586 M) DEEP.

" THE SCULPTED PILLARS AND VAULTED CEILINGS LOOK JUST LIKE THE INSIDE OF AN ORNATELY CARVED CATHEDRAL, BUT CARVED BY NATURE! "

# VALLE DE LA LUNA

## ATACAMA DESERT, CHILE

Towering peaks of rugged red rock have been carved into dramatic shapes by the wind. Around them, bright white salt lies in drifts like snow, up to 1.6 ft. (0.5 m) thick.

Valle de la Luna has been dry for 150 million years, but it's not especially hot. Its dryness is the result of its position. The Andes Mountains shield it from rain coming from the east, and cold water rising from the Pacific Ocean on the west creates conditions where water doesn't evaporate to form rain clouds.

### LIFE IN THE DESERT

Not even insects can survive in the driest core of the desert, but some microbes do manage to live here. They are adapted to hyper-dry conditions, so when it does very infrequently rain, these microbes are killed.

Astrobiologists—people who study the possibility of life elsewhere in space—study the microbes that survive here as they might reveal how life could tolerate conditions on other planets. Mars rovers are tested here, too! Looking around at this otherworldly environment, it's no surprise to learn that Valle de la Luna means "valley of the moon."

> " THE ATACAMA DESERT IS THE DRIEST DESERT ON EARTH (EXCEPT FOR THE ICE DESERT OF ANTARCTICA); SOME PARTS HAVE HAD NO RAINFALL IN 100 YEARS, OR AVERAGE ONLY 0.04 IN. (1 MM) A YEAR. "

**THE HIGH ALTITUDE AND CLOUDLESS SKIES MAKE THE ATACAMA DESERT PERFECT FOR STARGAZING!**

NASA scientists come here to practice searching for life on Mars.

THE ATACAMA DESERT IS THE OLDEST DESERT ON EARTH—IT'S BEEN DRY FOR 150 MILLION YEARS!

# THE GALÁPAGOS ISLANDS

## OFF THE COAST OF ECUADOR

This collection of 127 remote islands scattered in the Pacific Ocean is home to unique creatures that are found nowhere else in the world. Only four of the islands are inhabited by humans.

The volcanic islands have emerged where three plates of the Earth's crust join and complex ocean currents meet. At 620 miles (1,000 km) off the coast of Ecuador, they are too distant for most animals to swim to. The animals here have evolved from ancestors that could fly or were blown by the wind or carried on floating debris across the water. The close interaction of sea and land has produced creatures that depend on both.

### LIFE ON THE ISLANDS

The only marine iguana in the world lives here. It has razor-sharp teeth that can scrape algae and seaweed from coastal

rocks. Elsewhere, iguanas eat leaves. The marine iguana sneezes out excess salt through a gland near its nose, and the salt then crystallizes into a cap on its head. It has long, curved claws for clinging to the rocks and holding firm in strong currents, and a flattened tail that helps it move through the water.

**THESE ARE SOME OF THE MOST REMOTE AND YOUNGEST ISLANDS ON EARTH; THE OLDEST IS 4.2 MILLION YEARS OLD.**

The male great frigatebird has a red throat pouch it inflates to attract a mate.

**THE MARINE IGUANA USES ITS LONG TAIL TO PROPEL ITSELF THROUGH THE WATER.**

# POSTOJNA CAVE

A cold, dark, underground world of caves lies beneath the limestone hills of Postojna in Slovenia. Towers of glistening rock make an unearthly spectacle.

A secret maze of rivers links cavernous halls and soaring pillars in an underground network 15 miles (24 km) long. This area of hills forms a type of landscape called karst. It was formed as water slowly dissolved the soft limestone rock to create caves.

Rainwater sinks into the ground and through the rock, then drips from the roof of a cave. Over hundreds of thousands of years, it deposits minerals, drip by drip, building fantastic stalagmites and stalactites up to 52 ft. (16 m) long.

## LIFE IN THE CAVE

The strangest animal here is the olm, or proteus, an amphibian. In the dark it needs no eyes, so it has lost them. There is little food deep in the caves, but that doesn't bother the olm. It can live for 10 years without eating and can even reabsorb parts of its own body if it's starving.

> " **THIS UNDERGROUND ENVIRONMENT IS PERPETUALLY DARK. "**

Olms (also called baby dragons) can live for more than 100 years!

PREDJAMA CASTLE WAS BUILT INTO THE ROCK ABOVE THE CAVE SYSTEM.

ELECTRIC LIGHTS WERE INSTALLED IN THE POSTOJNA CAVES IN 1884, BEFORE MANY OF EUROPE'S CAPITAL CITIES HAD ELECTRIC LIGHTS!

# FINGAL'S CAVE

## STAFFA, SCOTLAND

Fierce waves batter a tower of volcanic rock off the coast of Scotland. Over millions of years, endlessly beaten by storms and harsh tides, the sea has carved an extraordinary cave into the rock.

The rocky island is formed of huge six-sided pillars of basalt. The rock formed strangely regular hexagonal columns as it cooled and hardened in the cold air and sea 60 million years ago. Today, waves crash against the cliff face and cascade into Fingal's Cave.

The flat top of the island is too exposed and bleak for large plants like trees, but grass and low-growing plants take root in the soil, and lichen clings to the rock by the entrance of the cave.

## LIFE ON THE ROCK

Seabirds such as guillemots and razorbills nest on the cliffs, safe from predators and high above the crashing sea. Puffins (pictured, below left) make burrows in the soil, sheltering themselves, their eggs, and their chicks from the fierce wind. In the past, people took sheep by boat to graze the island in the summer, but now it is uninhabited and kept safe for wildlife.

GUILLEMOTS SPEND MOST OF THEIR LIVES AT SEA, ONLY COMING ASHORE TO NEST ON THE CLIFFS.

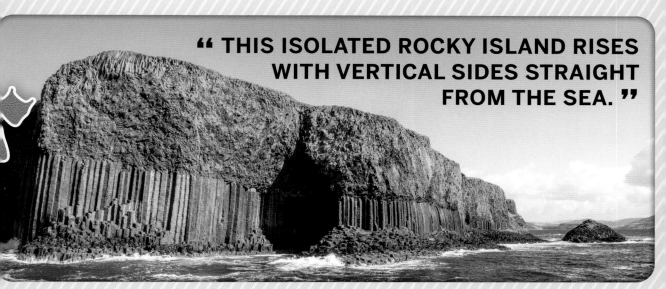

**" THIS ISOLATED ROCKY ISLAND RISES WITH VERTICAL SIDES STRAIGHT FROM THE SEA. "**

Waves pummel the rocks, splashing 130 ft. (40 m) up the cliff.

# DIAMOND BEACH AND
## JÖKULSÁRLÓN GLACIER LAGOON

### JÖKULSÁRLÓN, ICELAND

Chunks of ice glittering like giant diamonds lie scattered over the jet-black sand of Diamond Beach and crowd the lagoon of Jökulsárlón. The ice is more than 1,000 years old and began as icebergs, shed into a lagoon by the Breiðamerkurjökull glacier.

Icebergs 100 ft. (30 m) high break away from the glacier where it enters the lagoon. They are carried out to sea to be tossed and polished by the waves. Then they drift ashore and become stranded on the volcanic sand.

The Jökulsárlón lagoon appeared in 1934 as the glacier began to retreat. Icebergs, some the size of apartment buildings, jostle in the crowded water. The lagoon fills the gap between the glacier and the Atlantic Ocean, growing as the glacier shrinks. The mix of fresh and salty water prevents it from freezing in winter.

### LIFE IN THE LAGOON

Seals shelter in the lagoon, where the water is calmer than the sea and where they are safe from predators such as whales. They go to the mouth of the lake to catch fish in winter.

BREIÐAMERKURJÖKULL IS PART OF EUROPE'S LARGEST GLACIER, VATNAJÖKULL, WHICH COVERS 3,050 SQUARE MILES (7,900 SQ KM).

" SOME OF THE ICE 'DIAMONDS' ARE BRIGHT BLUE OR EVEN HAVE STREAKS OF BLACK VOLCANIC ASH RUNNING THROUGH THEM. "

THE JÖKULSÁRLÓN LAGOON IS ICELAND'S DEEPEST LAKE, AT 814 FT. (248 M) DEEP.

# BIAŁOWIEŻA FOREST

## POLAND & BELARUS

This huge, dense green forest on the border between Poland and Belarus shelters animals that have been driven out of other parts of Europe by human actions. It is the last remnant of Europe's ancient forest, and a glimpse of how most of northern Europe looked long ago.

The forest grew 8,000 years ago and had no human inhabitants until 600 years ago. For a long time, the only way to pass through the impenetrable growth was by boat along the few waterways. The forest was kept as a royal hunting ground, so it remained wild and full of animals.

### LIFE IN THE FOREST

The last surviving herd of European bison lives in the forest. Now numbering 800 animals, they were reintroduced after the last wild bison were killed around 1920.

Other thriving creatures include wild horses, deer, elk, wolves, wild boar, and lynx (pictured, right), which all live among the oak and lime trees, along with birds, small mammals, and amphibians.

Over half the wood in the forest is dead; it supports 12,000 types of organisms that feed on dead wood.

**THIS IS THE LARGEST ANCIENT FOREST IN EUROPE, AT 1,190 SQUARE MILES (3,086 SQ KM).**

" **THE OLDEST TREES ARE MORE THAN 500 YEARS OLD; THE LARGEST IS NEARLY 23 FT. (7 M) AROUND THE TRUNK.** "

MALE EURASIAN WOLVES SWALLOW FOOD, THEN REGURGITATE IT FOR THEIR PUPS TO EAT!

WILD BOAR ARE NOCTURNAL: THEY FORAGE AT NIGHT AND REST IN THE DAY.

The very dense forest growth keeps the environment isolated.

# CHERNOBYL DISASTER SITE

## PRIPYAT, UKRAINE

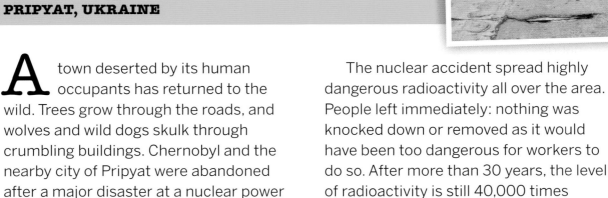

A town deserted by its human occupants has returned to the wild. Trees grow through the roads, and wolves and wild dogs skulk through crumbling buildings. Chernobyl and the nearby city of Pripyat were abandoned after a major disaster at a nuclear power plant in 1986.

The nuclear accident spread highly dangerous radioactivity all over the area. People left immediately: nothing was knocked down or removed as it would have been too dangerous for workers to do so. After more than 30 years, the level of radioactivity is still 40,000 times higher than normal. The region will

**IT IS THE LARGEST AREA OF "REWILDING" IN EUROPE: THE LACK OF PEOPLE HAS INCREASED BIODIVERSITY.**

probably lie unusable for 20,000 years—twice the length of human civilization so far!

### LIFE IN THE FOREST

Packs of wild dogs hunt in the deserted settlement, the descendants of pet dogs left behind by people fleeing the disaster.

Radioactivity can cause cancer and mutations (mistakes in a growing plant or animal). The young of animals exposed to radiation often have something wrong with them, but life around Chernobyl is surviving despite the dangers.

**" VERY HIGH LEVELS OF RADIOACTIVITY MAKE THE AREA DEADLY DANGEROUS. "**

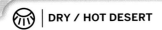
# THE NAMIB DESERT AND
# SKELETON COAST

## COAST OF NAMIBIA

**IN SOME PLACES, THE RED SAND CONTRASTS STARKLY WITH BRIGHT WHITE SALT LEFT BY DRIED-UP RIVERBEDS.**

Stretching along the Atlantic coast of Namibia, the oldest desert in the world is often wreathed in fog. The Skeleton Coast is littered with the wrecks of ships grounded in the fog, giving it its sinister name.

The Namib has been a desert for between 55 and 80 million years. A traditional sandy desert, it has the second-largest sand dunes in the world, 980 ft. (300 m) high and 20 miles (32 km) long. They provide a vast, empty landscape with no shade or shelter. It is some of the driest land on Earth, with virtually no rain, freezing by night and scorching by day.

### LIFE IN THE DESERT

Plants and animals have adapted to survive on the water of the fog near the coast. The living-fossil plant Welwitschia collects water on its leaves and can live up to 2,000 years. Black-backed jackals (right) lick stones to drink water condensed from the air. Darkling beetles have micro-bumps on their wings to trap water from fog and trickle it toward their mouths.

" THE SKELETON COAST HAS 180 DAYS OF FOG A YEAR. "

THE STRANGE WELWITSCHIA PLANT IS TOTALLY UNIQUE AND DEPENDS ON FOG FOR SURVIVAL.

The daytime temperature reaches 113°F (45°C).

# ᵀʜᴇ DANAKIL DEPRESSION

## DALLOL, ETHIOPIA

Pools of scalding, brilliant blue-green water stud a hellishly hot and bizarre landscape. Among the hottest inhabited places on Earth, Dallol is heated from below by volcanic activity, and the land is being slowly torn apart at 0.4–0.8 in. (1–2 cm) a year. It's no surprise this area is called the "Gateway to Hell."

Over millions of years, Africa will break in two along a line that runs through Dallol. Nearby, open craters form lakes of bubbling hot lava, showing the underground turmoil. The Awash River flows into the Danakil Depression, making lakes that evaporate to leave saltpans and a crust of brightly colored mineral crystals.

### LIFE AMONG THE CRATERS

The earliest humans probably evolved nearby, 3.2 million years ago. Now, the Afar people live here, collecting salt to sell. Well adapted to hot, dry conditions, they need less food and water than most people. Near ground level, the level of carbon dioxide (a heavy gas) is too high for animals to survive, so only taller animals and birds can live here.

**DALLOL HAS THE WORLD'S HIGHEST AVERAGE YEAR-ROUND TEMPERATURE, AT 94°F (34.4°C).**

" THIS IS ONE OF THE LOWEST
AREAS ON EARTH: 410 FT. (125 M)
BELOW SEA LEVEL. "

# VICTORIA FALLS ZAMBEZI RIVER

**BORDER OF ZIMBABWE & ZAMBIA**

TRUMPETER HORNBILLS MAKE A LOUD WAILING, NASAL CALL LIKE A CRYING BA[BY]

At Victoria Falls, one of the largest rivers in Africa cascades over a rocky cliff 354 ft. (108 m) high, crashing with a huge roar into the "Boiling Pot" at its base—a turbulent pool 230 ft. (70 m) deep. The water creates an enormous cloud of mist and spray, rising 1,300 ft. (400 m) into the air, and visible from up to 30 miles (48 km) away. The river then rushes away, finally reaching the Indian Ocean in Mozambique.

Water approaches the falls rushing at 25 mph (40 kph). At their widest, the falls are 1 mile (1.6 km) side to side, but in the dry season from April to September, they narrow, and the water volume shrinks. Drought can reduce the falls to a trickle.

## LIFE BY THE FALLS

Fish live in the river above and below the falls, attracting waterbirds that feed on them. Elephants wade and swim through the river above the waterfalls, going between islands to cross the river. At the top of the gorge, opposite the falls, a tropical rainforest has grown, watered by the constant mist produced by the spray. Birds and mammals thrive in the lush vegetation, including vervet monkeys, chacma baboons, and trumpeter hornbills.

IN THE WET SEASON, VICTORIA FALLS IS THE LARGEST WATERFALL IN THE WORLD. IT IS TWICE THE HEIGHT OF NIAGARA FALLS!

VERVET MONKEYS OFTEN LIVE NEAR RIVERS OR LAKES AND ARE GOOD SWIMMERS.

" **LOCAL PEOPLE CALL THE FALLS** *MOSI-OA-TUNYA,* **WHICH MEANS 'SMOKE THAT THUNDERS' IN THE BANTU LANGUAGE.** "

In the wet season, 145 million gallons of water flow over the falls every minute.

# SAHARA EL BEYDA
## (THE WHITE DESERT)

**FARAFRA, EGYPT**

U nearthly towers of creamy-white rock sculpted by the wind dot the White Desert. They have formed over hundreds of years as the chalk-rich rock has been sandblasted by the wind into bizarre shapes.

Some shapes have been given names, like "chicken and tree" or "ice-cream cone," because they remind people of these objects, but all have occurred naturally as sand carried by the wind has worn away the surface. By moonlight, the rocks glow a ghostly white. Eventually, the windblown sand will whisk away the rest of the rock.

Between the chalk spires, the sand is scattered with quartz crystals and deep-black iron pyrites. The area was a seabed millions of years ago, and small fossils of sea creatures lie in the sand.

### LIFE IN THE DESERT
With no soil, plants are unable to grow among the rocks, though scrubby desert plants and acacia trees grow around the edges of the desert.

**THE AREA IS WHIPPED BY FIERCE WINDS CARRYING SCOURING SAND.**

## " THE WHITE DESERT HAS LESS THAN 0.08 IN. (2 MM) OF RAIN A YEAR. "

**THIS NATURAL SCULPTURE—CALLED THE MUSHROOM ROCK—IS OVER 10 FT. (3 M) TALL.**

**WHALE FOSSILS FOUND HERE ARE FROM THE SEA THAT COVERED THIS AREA MILLIONS OF YEARS AGO.**

# MOUNT LICO

**ZAMBEZIA, MOZAMBIQUE**

T his isolated tropical forest, hidden on top of a mountain, is cut off from its surroundings by sheer, near-vertical cliffs. It was only discovered in satellite images in 2012, buried deep in the undisturbed forest of Mozambique.

The shortest route to the top is 410 ft. (125 m) high and can only be scaled by professional climbers. It was first visited by scientists in 2018 and there is still lots to discover about it. Local people knew the forest was there, but they could only look at it from below. For now, this mountain-forest and its history remain mysterious.

## LIFE AT THE TOP

For animals to get to the forest, they must fly or climb the rocks. Those spotted so far include lizards and small mammals, plus giant rats the size of cats. Surprisingly, there are no birds—but there are lots of spiders, caterpillars, and butterflies that would be eaten if there were birds! A few ancient handmade pots were found in the forest, showing that at least one person has been there before, but they haven't been dated yet.

**" THE HIDDEN FOREST IS SURROUNDED BY CLIFFS UP TO 2,300 FT. (700 M) HIGH AND NEARLY IMPENETRABLE WOODLAND. "**

THERE MAY BE A NEW SPECIES OF CAECILIAN
(A SNAKE-LIKE AMPHIBIAN) IN THE FOREST.

MANY FROGS LIVE HERE, INCLUDING
THE BREVICEPS FROG (OR RAIN FROG).

# ANKARANA
## NATIONAL PARK

**NORTHERN MADAGASCAR**

A land spiky with natural limestone towers hides a network of caves and underground rivers where crocodiles lurk. It ends at one edge with the Wall of Ankarana, a sheer cliff 15.5 miles (25 km) long.

The limestone karsts are relics of a landscape 150 million years old. It rains a lot here, and the water has dissolved parts of the limestone to leave jagged spires and ridges, and to cut gorges, caves, and channels for hidden rivers. The sharp, rocky pinnacles and hidden patches of forest are home to more primates than anywhere else in the world.

### LIFE AMONG THE ROCKS

Lemurs of many kinds climb through the rocks and dense trees. Giant bats live in one of the caves, and the world's only large cave crocodiles haunt the underground rivers. The Ambatoharanana "crocodile" cave is 11 miles (18 km) long—plenty of space for lots of crocodiles! The underground system includes pockets of isolated forest, and caves where bat droppings provide nourishment for water creatures that crocodiles can eat. Crocodiles are safe from human hunters in the caves, which might be why they live there.

> **" ANKARANA NATIONAL PARK CONTAINS THE LONGEST CAVE SYSTEM IN MADAGASCAR, AND PROBABLY IN ALL OF AFRICA. "**

The area receives 6.5 ft. (2 m) of rain a year!

# BAMBOO FOREST

## YIXING, CHINA

A forest with no trees sounds impossible—but here, the dense growth of towering bamboo crowds out almost all plants, and leaves no space for trees.

The bamboo forest is the world's largest natural monoculture (an area where one species dominates). Hardly anything else grows here, just a few grasses and ferns at ground level.

Bamboo looks like a tree, but it's actually a flowering grass. It's by far the largest grass and the fastest growing. Some types grow up to 35 in. (90 cm) in a single day and can be 100 ft. (30 m) tall! All the bamboo of one species, everywhere in the world, flowers and then dies at the same time, at intervals of 60–130 years. The stands of bamboo then have to regrow from seed.

### LIFE IN THE FOREST

When the bamboo dies, it's devastating for the animals that rely on it for food, such as the giant panda, which eats hardly anything else. It's terrible for humans, too. The sudden arrival of seed brings rats to the forest. When they've eaten the seeds, they turn to raiding people's grain stores, causing disease and food shortages.

---

**PANDAS SPEND UP TO 14 HOURS A DAY EATING AS MUCH AS 26 LB. (12 KG) OF BAMBOO.**

**SOME TYPES OF BAMBOO GROW SO FAST YOU CAN ALMOST WATCH THEM GROW! "**

This is the largest bamboo forest in China, covering 46 square miles (120 sq km).

# MAWSYNRAM

## MEGHALAYA, INDIA

This dense forest drips with warm rain, and rivers cascade through the lush undergrowth. Mawsynram is the wettest place on Earth and teems with plant and animal life. The name of the district, Meghalaya, means "abode of the clouds."

The tropical forest is drenched by the rain that falls between May and October. Nearly 23 ft. (7 m) of rain falls in June and July alone! The warm, wet climate and fertile soil support thousands of types of flowering plants and many trees, mosses, and ferns, making a rich, green world like no other.

### LIFE IN THE RAIN

Living with the rain is a challenge for the people of Mawsynram. Rushing water tears down structures, and wet air rots wood in a short space of time, so people weave bridges over the many rivers using living rubber trees. Their roots are trained around bamboo canes; by the time the canes have rotted, the roots are thick and self-supporting. The people themselves wear full body umbrellas, called *knups*, made of bamboo and banana leaf.

The humid forest is home to elephants, tigers, bisons, hoolock gibbons, boars, barking deer, sambars, leopards, apes, and monkeys.

HOOLOCK GIBBONS SWING QUICKLY FROM TREE TO TREE AND HARDLY EVER TOUCH THE GROUND.

**THIS IS THE WETTEST PLACE ON EARTH, WITH NEARLY 40 FT. (12 M) OF RAIN EACH YEAR!** "

KNUPS LEAVE THE WEARER'S HANDS FREE WHILE PROTECTING THEIR BODY FROM RAIN.

# THE LUT DESERT
## (DASHT-E LUT)

**IRAN**

H arsh winds whip sand through the scorching air, making vicious sandstorms in the Lut Desert. The storms sculpt dunes and rock into weird and unearthly shapes.

One of the hottest and driest places on Earth, the center of the desert has no soil and plants can't grow there. Although the river Rud-e Shur flows into the Lut, it is so salty that nothing grows along its banks—it remains as barren as the rest of the desert. The land is so hostile it is not even at risk from human activity; hardly anyone ever goes into the heart of the desert.

## LIFE IN THE DESERT

The largest animals are Rüppell's sand foxes, which hide in holes in the rocks in the heat of the day and come out at night. Their fragile food web seems to be supported by birds dying as they fly over the desert. Their bodies fall to the ground, where the desert wildlife can feed on them. Insects feed on the waste of the foxes and the birds' remains, and geckos eat the insects.

The highest surface temperature on Earth was recorded here: 159.3°F (70.7°C).

' THE WORLD'S HIGHEST SAND DUNES ARE HERE. "

# MOUNT EVEREST AND THE HIGH HIMALAYAS

## NEPAL & TIBET, CHINA

High in the Himalayas, a dry desert of snow and rock stretches to the tallest mountain peaks in the world. Whipped by ferocious winds and freezing temperatures, it's one of the most hostile environments on Earth.

There is little plant life and low levels of oxygen in the high mountains, making it hard for any animals to survive. Surfaces of bare, jagged rock crusted with snow and ice, sheer cliff faces, treacherous glaciers, and howling subzero blizzards try even the hardiest animals.

### LIFE ON THE MOUNTAINS

Yaks, snow leopards, and Bengal tigers have thick fur to keep them warm. The snow leopard has an unusually long tail that helps it balance on rocks, and can be wrapped around its body like a scarf. The yak has wide hooves for balance, and a very rough tongue, adapted to scraping lichen off rocks at altitudes where no plants grow. Its large lungs and heart allow it to survive low levels of oxygen.

The Himalayan jumping spider lives at the highest altitude (21,000 ft. / 6,300 m), feeding on insects blown up by the wind.

YAKS SHED THEIR WOOLLY UNDERCOATS IN SUMMER AND TIBETAN NOMADS TURN IT INTO A SOFT FABRIC.

" **THE HIMALAYAS ARE THE HIGHEST MOUNTAINS IN THE WORLD, WITH MOUNT EVEREST THE HIGHEST, AT 29,029 FT. (8,848 M).** "

SNOW LEOPARD

# THE DEAD SEA

## JORDAN, ISRAEL, & THE PALESTINIAN TERRITORIES

The deepest salt lake in the world is a vast expanse of poisonous water in the Jordan Rift Valley. The water of the Dead Sea is so salty that nothing can live in it, giving it its name.

The water is cut off from the ocean, so is not really a sea at all but a huge lake. And although it's officially labeled "freshwater," it's far from fresh. Rivers carry mineral salts from the surrounding land into the lake, and in the hot summer the water evaporates, leaving behind the salts. Over the course of 65,000 years, this has made the water more and more salty, crusting the shores and rocks with salt.

### LIFE IN THE LAKE

Only a tiny number of microscopic fungi and bacteria can survive in the water. Animals and plants swept into the Dead Sea with the river water all die. Yet the area has been used as a health resort for 2,000 years. People visit to lie in the health-giving mud of the shores, and to enjoy floating on the super-salty water, which easily buoys them up.

**AT 997 FT. (304 M) DEEP, IT'S THE DEEPEST SALT LAKE IN THE WORLD.**

> **" THE DEAD SEA HAS NEARLY NINE TIMES THE SALT CONCENTRATION OF OCEAN WATER. "**

# THE GANGES RIVER

## NORTHEASTERN INDIA

The longest river in India flows from melting glaciers in the Himalayas and is fed by monsoon rains on its path to the sea 1,550 miles (2,500 km) away. Running fast and furiously in the mountains, its passage is sluggish and steady over the plains.

The massive basin of the Ganges is home to 650 million people, making it the most populated river basin in the world. It is a holy river, revered by Hindus.

The river is under threat from human activity as people take water from the river more quickly than it is replenished and pollute it with all kinds of waste. Fishing and redirecting water to supply farmland and industry cause further damage.

### LIFE ON THE RIVER

The Ganges river dolphin lives only in the Ganges river system. Adapted to the muddy river, it has poor eyesight and searches the riverbed for food by swimming on its side and trailing a fin through the mud. People have used the river for drinking, bathing, transportation, and religious ceremonies (including ceremonies to dispose of their dead) for centuries. As it becomes more polluted, these activities become increasingly dangerous.

**" THE GANGES IS THE LONGEST RIVER IN INDIA, AT 1,550 MILES (2,500 KM). "**

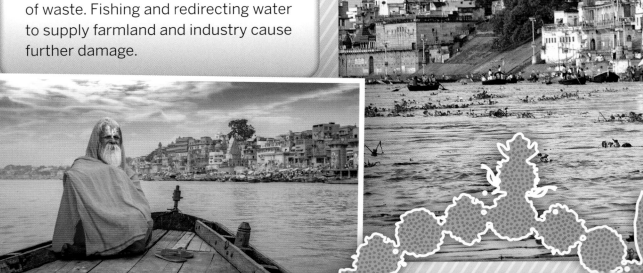

The river basin covers almost 400,000 square miles (1 million sq km).

# ANAK KRAKATAU

## INDONESIA

Anak Krakatau is a barren, blackened volcanic island in a region rich in lush tropical forests. It's all that's left of the island of Krakatau, completely destroyed by a huge volcanic eruption in 1883. A fringe of forest around the coast is the beginning of a new island ecosystem.

The new island rose from the sea, itself the result of volcanic activity, 80 years ago. It began as empty black rock, with volcanic ash and sand rather than soil. Seeds like coconuts and sea-almonds floated in on the sea and others were blown by the wind and began to grow. Most are around the coast, because continuing eruptions, heat, and poisonous gases make the interior a harsh environment.

### LIFE ON THE ISLAND

The land was completely lifeless after the massive eruption of 1883 but now has abundant life on the coast, including around 100 types of plants, plus birds and insects. Fig and other fruit trees have grown from seed in bird droppings. These then attracted passing birds and fed windblown insects, which have colonized the island.

**THE 1883 VOLCANIC ERUPTION WAS ONE OF THE BIGGEST EVER RECORDED—THE EXPLOSIONS WERE HEARD THOUSANDS OF MILES AWAY!**

"ANAK KRAKATAU IS STILL EXTREMELY VOLCANICALLY ACTIVE, WITH FIVE EVENTS BETWEEN 2009 AND 2019."

The island grew to 1,109 ft. (338 m) above sea level in just 90 years.

# KATI THANDA-
# LAKE EYRE

**SOUTH AUSTRALIA**

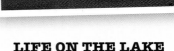

L ake Eyre (pronounced "air") is rarely there! It only floods with water about once every 10 years when there is enough rain, but it makes a big impact when it does.

Usually, the "lake" is a vast, dry salt flat. But when torrential rains come, streams and rivers drain into it. Most years, rain doesn't reach Lake Eyre, but sometimes it floods and just occasionally—about once every 50 years—it fills completely.

The lake water starts off fresh, because it's rainwater, and becomes salty as minerals from the lake bed dissolve in it. Algae grow in the mineral-rich water, producing amazing pink colors.

## LIFE ON THE LAKE

During dry years, the land looks dead, but the eggs of brine shrimp and fish lie buried, waiting for the water. When the lake floods, they hatch, grow, and breed. Flocks of waterbirds arrive to feast on them.

Most astonishingly, 100,000 pelicans fly here from the coast, setting out on their long journey before the rains even start! No one understands how they know when to come, but they never get it wrong. They breed on islands in the lake and raise their chicks here, where there is more food than at the coast.

> **"THIS IS THE WORLD'S LARGEST EPHEMERAL LAKE, MEANING IT LASTS ONLY FOR A SHORT TIME."**

**THIS PACIFIC GULL HAS COME TO FEAST ON CRUSTACEANS IN THE LAKE.**

The lake is the lowest point in Australia, up to 49 ft. (15 m) below sea level.

# FRANKLIN-GORDON WILD RIVERS NATIONAL PARK

## TASMANIA, AUSTRALIA

Lush, temperate forest covers ancient rocks that have been sculpted by ice and water over hundreds of millions of years. Beneath the greenery lies a landscape of dramatic cliffs, caves, plunging gorges, sinkholes, and cascading waterfalls.

The wilderness lies between two rivers, Franklin and Gordon, and is crossed by only a single road. Within its rugged and folded rock formations lie Australia's longest cave system, deepest cave, and deepest lake! It was part of a vast forest that split apart as lands shifted, leaving other remnants in New Zealand and Patagonia.

### LIFE IN THE WILDERNESS

The trees include towering giants such as the Huon pine that can live for 3,000 years and the swamp gum, the tallest flowering plant in the world, at up to 330 ft. (100 m) tall.

The varied animals include monotremes—a small and ancient group of mammals that lay eggs! Monotremes are found only in Australia and New Guinea. Here, the echidna scurries about the forest floor, and the duck-billed platypus (right) swims in the rivers.

**ECHIDNA**

THE RIVER REFLECTS THE BLUE SKY, BUT THE WATER IS THE COLOR OF WEAK TEA, STAINED BY CHEMICALS IN BUTTON GRASS GROWING WHERE THE WATER COLLECTS.

**" THIS IS ONE OF THE LARGEST AREAS OF UNTOUCHED TEMPERATE RAINFOREST IN THE WORLD, AT OVER 1,700 SQ. MILES (4,400 SQ KM). "**

# THE OUTBACK

## AUSTRALIA

This parched and remote land in the center of Australia is one of the largest remaining areas of natural wilderness on the planet. The scorching, bone-dry summer switches almost instantly to frosty winter, with little spring or fall.

The "red center" of the Outback is the hottest, driest region, with sand plains, salt pans, and usually only scrubby vegetation. Rain is unpredictable, but when it comes, lush plant growth springs from the dust.

### LIFE IN THE OUTBACK

Heat and dryness—and the raging wildfires they lead to—are the main challenges for wildlife here. Rain and dew collect on the skin of the thorny devil lizard and run in grooves to its mouth, so it doesn't miss a drop of valuable water. Plants including eucalyptus survive and even rely on wildfires, which clear land or prompt their seeds to grow.

Native Australian animals of the Outback include the red kangaroo, wallaby, dingo, and crocodile. The world's only wild herd of dromedaries (one-humped camels) lives in the Outback, though they are not native to Australia.

**THE DRIEST AREAS GET AT MOST 6 IN. (150 MM) OF RAIN A YEAR.**

**THE WILD CAMELS ARE DESCENDED FROM ANIMALS BROUGHT OVER FROM AFGHANISTAN.**

> **" THE TEMPERATURE VARIES WILDLY, FROM 18.5°F (-7.5°C) IN WINTER TO OVER 104°F (40°C) IN SUMMER. "**

The Outback covers 70 percent of the Australian continent.

# WAITOMO GLOWWORM CAVES

## NORTH ISLAND, NEW ZEALAND

A network of 300 dark, wet caves snakes through hills formed over 30 million years ago. Dazzling stalactites hang from cave roofs and stalagmites grow from the floors but, even more incredibly, some of the caves are illuminated by the eerie glow of millions of glowworms.

The rocks are limestone, first formed under the sea from compressed fossilized shells and fish skeletons in layers up to 655 ft. (200 m) thick. Volcanic activity moved and split the rock, and then water flowing through cracks dissolved the limestone to create caves. Minerals deposited from the water have made the spectacular towers of glittering stalactites and stalagmites, growing only 0.06 cubic inches (1 cubic centimeter) in 100 years.

### LIFE IN THE CAVES

The most dramatic inhabitants of the caves are the glowworms. Despite the name, they are not actually worms but the larvae (grubs) of a gnat and glow with blue-green light produced by chemicals in their bodies. Other insects adapted to the cold, dark, and damp include white albino cave ants and giant crickets. Eels live in some of the underground lakes.

**THE GLOWWORMS THAT LIGHT UP THE WAITOMO CAVES CAN BE FOUND ONLY IN NEW ZEALAND.**

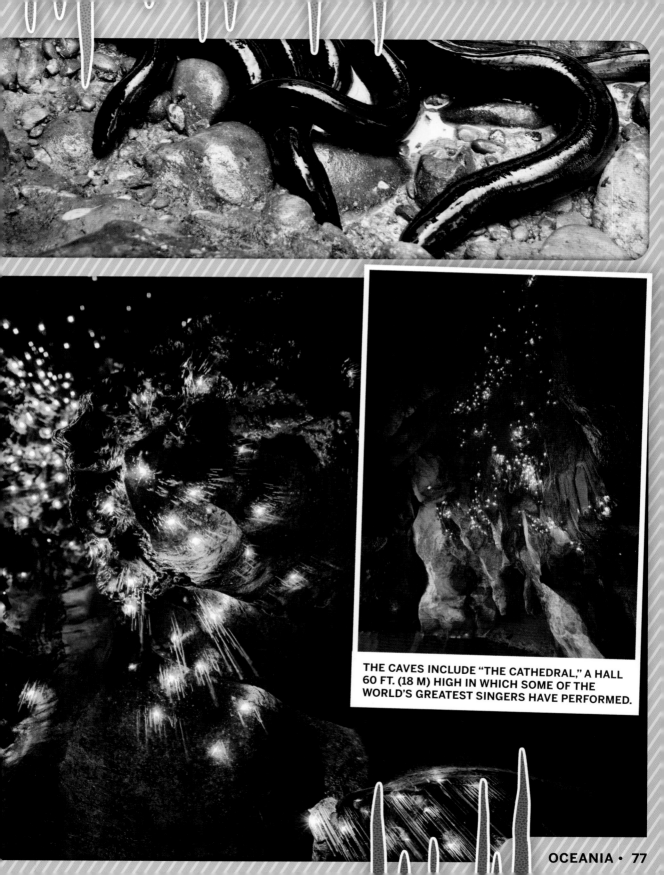

THE CAVES INCLUDE "THE CATHEDRAL," A HALL 60 FT. (18 M) HIGH IN WHICH SOME OF THE WORLD'S GREATEST SINGERS HAVE PERFORMED.

# TROPICAL FOREST

## PAPUA NEW GUINEA

One of the largest areas of tropical rainforest in the world is isolated on the island of Papua New Guinea. It's teeming with a rich diversity of plant and animal life, with no large predators to limit them.

Forty-four groups of uncontacted indigenous people live in Papua New Guinea, all with lifestyles perfectly adapted to the rainforest. But their way of life and homes are under threat as the forest around them is cut down for timber or burned to clear land for farming and mining.

### LIFE IN THE FOREST

In this crowded, closed ecosystem, animals and birds must specialize and distinguish themselves. Birds of paradise have grown spectacular, bright feathers to make the differences between species clear, helping them to find suitable mates.

Besides monotremes (egg-laying mammals), the forest has the flightless cassowary, one of the largest birds in the world. Growing 6.5 ft. (2 m) tall and weighing as much as 130 lb. (60 kg), it can run fast and deliver a deadly kick. There are also tree kangaroos, 760 bird species found nowhere else on Earth, and butterflies the size of birds.

**THE WETTEST AREAS RECEIVE 30 FT. (9 M) OF RAIN A YEAR.**

**" THIS AREA MAKES UP JUST 0.5 PERCENT OF THE EARTH'S SURFACE BUT CONTAINS 5–10 PERCENT OF ALL THE SPECIES ON THE PLANET! "**

FEMALE ECLECTUS PARROTS NEST IN HOLLOWS IN LARGE RAINFOREST TREES.

CASSOWARIES CAN RUN AT UP TO 30 MPH (50 KPH).

# ICE SHEET AND COAST

## ANTARCTICA

The Antarctic wilderness is one of the most desolate and beautiful landscapes on Earth. A frozen wasteland, land and sea are almost indistinguishable when the sea freezes each winter.

The continent of Antarctica, the land beneath the ice, is twice the size of Australia—yet 1,000–5,000 visiting scientists are the only people who live here.

The ice on the sea shifts and breaks up in the spring, revealing the coastline. Only moss and algae grow on the rocks here; there are no plants, birds, or animals.

The landscape is hidden beneath a blanket of white, with valleys filled by ice up to 2.5 miles (4 km) thick that has built up over hundreds of thousands of years. The tallest mountains, at over 15,000 ft. (4,500 m), poke through the ice sheet—the only exposed land away from the coast.

### LIFE ON THE ICE

Emperor penguins nest on the ice sheet in winter but never set foot on solid land. The ice cliffs and icebergs shelter them from the howling, freezing winds. Around the coast and islands of Antarctica, leopard seals, elephant seals, fur seals, and many varieties of penguins populate the beaches and ice floes.

" **THE OLDEST GLACIER FRAGMENTS ARE 15 MILLION YEARS OLD.** "

THE WORLD'S COLDEST RECORDED TEMPERATURE IS IN ANTARCTICA, A BONE-CHILLING -128.6°F (-89.2°C).

Emperor penguins can swim underwater for up to 20 minutes!

# BLOOD FALLS

## MCMURDO DRY VALLEYS, ANTARCTICA

**B**lood appears to seep down sheer cliffs of ice, jarring with the frozen landscape. This terrifying terrain is the dry McMurdo desert of Antarctica.

The waterfall, five stories high, is fed by a lake deep within the Taylor glacier. The water has been hidden 1,300 ft. (400 m) under the ice for millions of years. It's much saltier than the sea—too salty to freeze—and very rich in iron. When it seeps through the ice and meets air for the first time, the iron rusts, turning the water the color of blood. It coats the rocks below, making a truly gory scene.

## LIFE ON THE ICE

Microbes in the glacier live by breaking down chemicals in the water. They have been cut off from the rest of the world for at least two million years and developed alone, with no light or heat.

The surrounding land is almost lifeless, with no trees and just two types of flowering plant. The only animals are tiny bugs such as springtails, mites, and tardigrades ("water bears"), just a fraction of an inch long.

**THE TEMPERATURE IS EXTREMELY COLD: -18°F–32°F (-28°C–0°C).**

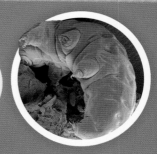

Microscopic tardigrades are also called "water bears" or "moss piglets."

## " BLOOD FALLS IS DARK THROUGHOUT THE POLAR WINTER AND LIGHT ALL SUMMER. "

**IT IS ONE OF THE DRIEST PLACES ON EARTH, WITH VERY LITTLE SNOWFALL.**

# SARGASSO SEA

## NORTH ATLANTIC OCEAN

The only sea defined by currents in the ocean rather than land boundaries, this warm patch of water has dense mats of sargassum seaweed that provide a surface rich in animal life. About 1,000 miles (1,600 km) wide and 3,000 miles (4,800 km) long, the Sargasso Sea is trapped within a clockwise-turning set of currents. Its swirling waters drag in anything passing—including massive amounts of debris and trash humans have dumped in the sea.

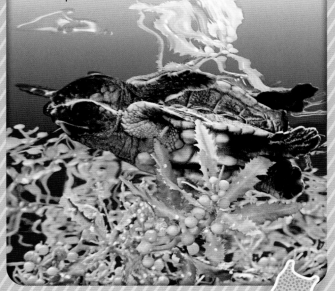

Sargassum is the only seaweed that can reproduce at the sea's surface—all others begin life on the seabed. Separated from the surrounding water by currents, the seaweed mats are trapped and can't drift away. They provide food and shelter on the ocean's surface. Turtle hatchlings, shrimp, and crabs crawl through them, and migrating seabirds and tuna feast on the animals that live there.

" **THIS IS THE ONLY SEA IN THE WORLD WITH NO LAND BOUNDARY.** "

## LIFE IN THE WEEDS

European eels migrate to the Sargasso Sea from the rivers and wetlands of Europe, where they live most of their lives. They spawn (produce their young) in the sea: leaf-shaped, transparent larvae that look nothing like eels! Over nearly a year, they make their way back across the ocean to Europe, where they might live for 80 years before returning to the Sargasso Sea to spawn and then die.

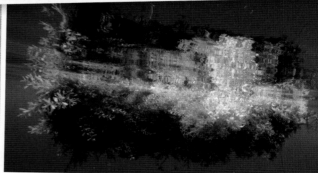

**MORE AND MORE SARGASSUM BLOOMS EVERY YEAR AS CLIMATE CHANGE AND HUMAN ACTIONS ALTER THE OCEAN'S CHEMISTRY AND TEMPERATURE.**

**SEABIRDS, INCLUDING THE WILLET, FEAST ON INSECTS IN THE SARGASSUM SEAWEED.**

# DEEP-SEA HYDROTHERMAL VENTS

Scorching acidic water at very high pressure pours from towering rocky columns deep in the ocean. Heated by volcanic activity below the seabed, the vent makes a bizarre environment where strange creatures live in conditions that would kill most forms of life.

Plates of the Earth's crust are pulling apart beneath the sea, with hot magma welling up to form new rock. Where water seeps into cracks in the seabed, it is heated to high temperatures and dissolves minerals from the volcanic rock. As it returns to the sea, it deposits the minerals, growing columns up to 200 ft. (60 m) tall. These are hydrothermal vents, which belch scalding water and gases into the sea.

## LIFE AT THE VENT

The mineral-rich water is too acidic and hot for most marine life. Organisms around the vents are called extremophiles, adapted to the extreme conditions here. Pompeii worms grow a colony of bacteria on their back that makes them appear hairy and provides insulation to protect them against the heat. Life here is based on using energy from chemicals, while ecosystems elsewhere use sunlight to provide energy.

**GIANT TUBE WORMS LIVE NEAR HYDROTHERMAL VENTS AND CAN GROW UP TO 8 FT. (2.4 M) LONG.**

" WATER AT 752°F (400°C) BLASTS INTO THE SEA UNDER HUGE PRESSURE, MAKING THE SEA NEARBY AS ACIDIC AS VINEGAR. "

# BAFFIN BAY

## ARCTIC & ATLANTIC OCEANS

This freezing sea is covered nearly all year by a white crust of ice. Icebergs break from ice sheets and glaciers, groaning and crunching as they grind against each other.

For most of the year, the sea forms a solid surface of ice, but in summer, a patch of 30,000 square miles (80,000 sq km) melts, freeing a passage to the north. The same area has been melting and refreezing for 9,000 years!

### LIFE AROUND THE ICE

The Greenland shark is the only shark to live under the ice sheets. It has specially adapted blood and body tissues to cope with greater water pressure at depth, because it dives down to warmer water far below the ice. Above, walruses and seals raise their pups on the ice. Sea mammals such as these, and the beluga whales and narwhals that live in the ice-free areas of sea, have thick blubber to keep them warm.

Inuit live on the Canadian side of the bay, hunting for fish and sea mammals. They get vitamin C from narwhal skin as no fruit or vegetables grow on the land.

**JUST 4–10 IN. (100–250 MM) OF RAIN/SNOW FALLS EACH YEAR, AS LITTLE AS IN A DESERT.**

The sea is frozen for nine months of the year.

**" HERE, THE AVERAGE WINTER TEMPERATURE IS −18.4°F (−28°C). "**

# GREAT BARRIER REEF

## AUSTRALIAN COAST & ISLANDS

Beneath the warm, shallow seas off the coast of Australia, hosts of brightly colored sea creatures swirl around the largest coral reef in the world. Intricate and beautiful structures of branching coral provide a rich and vibrant ecosystem like nowhere else on Earth.

The reef has been built by billions of microscopic animals, called coral polyps, over 25 million years. The animals make a tiny hard casing to live in, building one on another to make massive structures that spread along the eastern coast of Australia.

There are 600 different types of hard and soft coral, making a varied and colorful scene. Yet pollution, climate change, and damage from shipping are harming the reef, leaving vast areas of dead, white coral.

### LIFE ON THE REEF

The reef is alive with brightly colored fish, shrimp, squid, sea stars, mollusks (like sea slugs), and other animals, including sea snakes, turtles, dolphins, and even crocodiles. Some, like mollusks and sea stars, clean the reef, and others form a complex food web by eating one another.

" THE GREAT BARRIER REEF ACCOUNTS FOR ONE-TENTH OF ALL THE REEF SYSTEMS IN THE WORLD, WITH 3,000 INDIVIDUAL REEFS AND 900 ISLANDS! "

The reef is the largest on Earth, covering an area of nearly 135,000 square miles (350,000 sq km).

# SALTSTRAUMEN MAELSTROM

## OFF THE COAST OF BODO, NORWAY

The strongest tidal current in the world swirls around a narrow gap off the coast of Norway, dividing a fjord (inlet) from the sea. It makes a maelstrom —a whirlpool of such extreme force it can be deadly to anyone who enters it.

As it flows in and out, the tide is forced through a very narrow channel, 1.9 miles (3 km) long and only 500 ft. (150 m) wide at the entrance to a fjord. A huge amount of water—110 billion gallons— rushes through the small gap every six hours, producing powerful whirlpools and swirling vortices. Some are 33 ft. (10 m) across and 16 ft. (5 m) deep at their center, pulling in anything snatched from the edge of their currents. The maelstrom has been raging four times a day, at every high and low tide, for 2,000 years. Between the tides, the channel is calm, and boats can safely travel between the sea and the fjord.

### LIFE IN THE MAELSTROM
The churning, turbulent water is a good environment for plankton (tiny living organisms). This attracts fish that eat the plankton, and then seabirds come to feed on the fish.

**WATER SPEEDS REACH 23 MPH (37 KPH)!**

# GLOSSARY

**ACIDIC –** with a chemical composition that can eat away other substances

**AMPHIBIAN –** animal that has wet skin, lays eggs in water, and lives in water during its phase as a young, immature form, but breathes air on land as an adult

**ANCESTORS –** previous generations, including grandparents and going backward through time

**ANCHORED –** securely fastened to a firm surface

**BASIN –** large dip in the land

**BUOY –** hold up in water

**CLIMATE –** long-term pattern of temperature and weather

**CLIMATE CHANGE –** changes in the climate, making the world hotter with more extreme weather events

**COLONY –** group of organisms that live together

**COMPETITION –** struggle between organisms for living space, food, water, or mates

**CONCENTRATED –** with a high proportion of something in one place

**CONDENSE –** turn from a gas to a liquid through cooling

**CRUST –** outer surface of Earth, made of solid rock. All the continents and oceans are part of the crust.

**CRYSTALLIZE –** form into solid crystals, blocks with a regular shape

**CURRENT –** flow of a stream of air or water in a particular direction

**DEHYDRATION –** drying out

**DORMANT –** not currently active

**ECOSYSTEM –** set of organisms and conditions interacting and existing together

**EPHEMERAL –** existing only briefly

**EQUATOR –** imaginary line that goes around the world, halfway between the North and South Poles. The hottest areas of Earth are near the equator.

**ERODE –** to wear away by the action of water, wind, abrasion (rubbing) by sand, stones, or ice

**EVAPORATE –** to turn from water to gas through heating

**EVOLVE / EVOLUTION –** the change in organisms over a long time as they adapt to the conditions in which they live or changes in those conditions

**FERTILE (LAND) –** good for growing plants as it contains nutrients

**FJORD –** long, narrow area of water connected to the sea and produced by a glacier

**FLASH FLOOD –** sudden flood of water caused by lots of rain falling in a short time

**FORAGE –** to move around looking for food

**FOSSILS –** remains or traces of living organisms preserved as or in rocks

**FUNGI –** organisms such as yeast and mushrooms that take their energy from chemicals in the surface they grow on, not from sunlight as plants do

**GLACIAL –** relating to ice

**GLACIER –** large bulk of ice that flows very slowly, like a frozen river

**HORIZON –** the apparent line where the land and sky meet

**HOSTILE –** unfriendly; with conditions that make it difficult to survive

**HUMID –** when lots of moisture is carried in the air

**HYDROTHERMAL –** with very hot water

**IMPENETRABLE –** impossible to get through

**INDUSTRIAL –** relating to industry, the processes, buildings, and machinery used to make things

**INSULATION –** layer of some substance that doesn't let heat through, so keeps things hot or cold for a long time

**KARST –** landscape made mostly of limestone, which forms underground channels and streams and often has towering hills or rocky columns

**LAVA –** very hot, molten rock from within Earth

**LIMESTONE –** a rock made of the bodies of prehistoric (extremely old) marine creatures, crushed over millions of years

**MAGMA –** very hot, semi-solid molten rock beneath Earth's crust

**MELTWATER –** water produced by melting ice

**MICROBE –** organisms so small they can only be seen with a microscope

**MICROSCOPIC –** so small that it can only be seen with a microscope

**MINERAL –** hard substance that forms a regular shape. Many minerals are rocks or are found in rocks.

**MONSOON –** torrential rain that falls in a wet season in some parts of the world

**NICHE –** restricted set of conditions in which an organism can live

**NUTRIENT –** chemical needed for growth

**PHOSPHOROUS –** chemical needed by plants and animals

**PLAINS –** large open expanses of grassland

**PLATE (TECTONIC) –** chunk of Earth's crust

**POLLUTE –** add to the environment chemicals, smoke, loud noise, extra light, trash, or anything else that causes harm

**PREDATOR –** animals that hunt and eat other animals

**PRIMATE –** group of animals that includes apes, monkeys, and human beings

**PYRITE (OR IRON PYRITE) –** yellowish mineral that looks a bit like gold

**QUARTZ –** very common type of mineral that forms large crystals that are often white but can be colored with other chemicals

**REFLECTIVE –** producing a reflection, like a mirror

**REGURGITATE –** bring back up after eating

**REMNANT –** remaining piece

**REPLENISH –** provide some more of something, renewing the supply

**SCOURING** – wearing away by rubbing with sand or some other abrasive material

**STALACTITE** – spike of minerals hanging down from the roof of a cave, deposited by mineral-rich water dripping over a long time

**STALAGMITE** – spike of minerals growing up from the floor of a cave, deposited by mineral-rich water

**SUBTROPICAL** – close to but outside the tropics, a band around the equator

**SUSTAINABLE** – produced in a way that doesn't damage the environment or use up things that can't be replaced

**THORNSCRUB** – hot, dry land with low, scrubby bushes and few trees

**TRIBE** – group of people who live together in a particular region and have their own identity, patterns of behavior, and customs

**TURMOIL** – disruption and chaotic activity

**UPSTREAM** – toward the source of a river or stream

**VOLCANO** – area where hot magma and gases from within Earth come out as lava. Some volcanoes are mountains, but others are splits or holes in the ground.

**VORTICES (VORTEX)** – whirling pools that pull water in and downward

---

The publisher would like to thank the following for their kind permission to reproduce their photographs:

**(Key: a-above; b-below; c-center; f-far; l-left; r-right; t-top)**

**Front cover** (l) Shutterstock / Daniel Prudek, (c) Shutterstock / Delbars, (r) Shutterstock / Avijan Saha; **Back cover** (tl) Shutterstock / City Escapes Nature Photo, (tc) Shutterstock / Barbara Ash, (tr) Shutterstock / Yvonne Baur, (br) Shutterstock / Aleksandra H. Kossowska, (bc) Shutterstock / Maythee Voran, (bl) Shutterstock / Barbara Ash, (cl) Shutterstock / Marcin Szymczak; **Page 3** (bl) Shutterstock / VarnaK, (bc) Shutterstock / Deni_Sugandi, (br) Getty Images / Tadej Zupancic; **Page 4** (br) Shutterstock / Bill Perry; **Page 5** (bl) Shutterstock / Claudio Soldi; **Page 6** (ca) Shutterstock / block23; (br) Shutterstock / Yvonne Baur; **Page 7** (crb) Shutterstock / FloridaStock, (br) Alamy / Nature Picture Library; **Page 8** (t) Shutterstock / block23, (crb) Shutterstock / Ondrej Prosicky, (br) Shutterstock / NON GG; **Page 9** (br) Shutterstock/ Arne Beruldsen; **Page 10** (t) Shutterstock / block23, (tr) Shutterstock / Luc Kohnen, (b) Shutterstock / Shane Myers Photography; **Page 11** (tr) Shutterstock / vagabond54, (b) Shutterstock / Juancat; **Page 12** (tr) Shutterstock / You Touch Pix of EuToch, (ca) Shutterstock / xpixel, (b) Shutterstock / Anton Foltin; **Page 13** (t) Shutterstock / Anton Foltin, (clb) Shutterstock/ Vaclav Sebek, (bl) Shutterstock /Dennis W Donohue, (br) Shutterstock / Martin Froyda; **Page 14** (tl) Shutterstock / block23, (tr) Shutterstock / Menno Schaefer; **Page 14/15** (b) Shutterstock / digidreamgrafix; **Page 15** (tr) Shutterstock / Cody_A, (cl) Shutterstock / Wildnerdpix, (cr) Shutterstock / FloridaStock; **Page 16** (tr) Shutterstock / Ruslan Kalnitsky; **Page 16-17** (b) Shutterstock / Lucky-photographer; **Page 17** (tl) Shutterstock / Andrea Izzotti, (tr) Shutterstock / Kyle Spradley Photography, (cra) Shutterstock / xpixel; **Page 18** (tr) Shutterstock / Sara_2021, (ca) Shutterstock / Makhh, (bl) Shutterstock / Wandering Otter; **Page 19** (tr) Shutterstock / Avijan Saha, (ca) Shutterstock / ScottBrownPhoto, (bl) Shutterstock / Leonardo Mercon, (br) Shutterstock / NON GG; **Page 20** (tr) Shutterstock / Angel DiBilio, (tl) Shutterstock / xpixel; **Page 20-21** (b) Shutterstock / Ernst Prettenthaler; **Page 21** (cla) Shutterstock / Dominic Gentilcore PhD, (tr) Shutterstock / canadastock, (br) Shutterstock / Angel DiBilio; **Page 22** (tr) Shutterstock / Claudio Soldi, (bl) Shutterstock / Loredana Habermann, (ca) Shutterstock / block23, (br) Shutterstock / T photography; **Page 23** Shutterstock / shinnji; **Page 24** (t) Shutterstock / block23, (crb) Shutterstock / Ondrej Prosicky, (br) Shutterstock / Kipling Brock; **Page 25** (t) Getty Images / Moment / LeoFFreitas, (bl) Alamy / Minden Pictures, (br) Shutterstock / Wonderly Imaging; **Page 26** (tr) Shutterstock / VarnaK, (cla) Shutterstock / block23; **Page 26-27** (b) Shutterstock / Jorge Ivan Vasquez C; **Page 28** (cla) Shutterstock / block23; **Page 28-29** (c ) Shutterstock / Alberto Loyo; **Page 29** (tr) Shutterstock / Ricardo_Dias; **Page 30** (tl) Shutterstock / xpixel, (bl) Shutterstock / xpixel, (br) Shutterstock / Skreidzeleu; **Page 30-31** (c) Shutterstock / Skreidzeleu; **Page 31** (tl) Shutterstock / Damian Gil, (tr) NASA CampoAlto/V. Robles; **Page 32** (tl) Shutterstock / block23, (tr) Shutterstock / wildestanimal; **Page 33** (cl) Shutterstock / Smileus, (tr) Shutterstock / Don Mammoser, (cr) Getty Images / iStock / MakingSauce, (crb) Shutterstock / RPBaiao; **Page 32-33** (b) Shutterstock / Rene Holtslag; **Page 34** (tl) Shutterstock / xpixel, (tl) Shutterstock / xpixel, (tr) Shutterstock / John_Silver; **Page 34-35** (b) Shutterstock / VIIIPhotography; **Page 35** (t) Shutterstock / Littleaom, (tr) Getty Images / E+ / Matjaz Slanic, (cr) Shutterstock / VIIIPhotography; **Page 36** (tr) Shutterstock / block23, (cr) Shutterstock / Simon Guettier, (b) Shutterstock / Milan Zygmunt; **Page 37** (t) Shutterstock / PaulienDam, (cra) Shutterstock / Ewan Chesser, (b) Shutterstock / Donna Carpenter; **Page 38** (cla) Shutterstock / block23; **Page 38-39** (tc) Shutterstock / Franco Fratini, (bc) Shutterstock / Jag_cz; **Page 39** (cra) Shutterstock / Viktorishy; **Page 40** (tr) Shutterstock / bchyla, (c ) Shutterstock / Makhh, (bc) Shutterstock / Bildagentur Zoonar GmbH, (br) Getty Images / iStock / Getty Images Plus / taviphoto; **Page 41** (c ) Getty Images / iStock / Getty Images Plus / Aleksander, (br) Shutterstock / Rudmer Zwerver; **Page 42** (tl) Shutterstock / Makhh, (tr) Shutterstock / BPTU, (clb) Shutterstock / ByBatman; **Page 42-43** (b) Shutterstock / Fotokon; **Page 43** (tc) Shutterstock / Sergiy Romanyuk, (cla) Shutterstock / Makhh, (cra) Shutterstock / EnolaBrain81; **Page 44** (tl) Shutterstock / xpixel, (tr) Shutterstock / Radek Borovka; **Page 44-45** (c ) Shutterstock / Maxim Babenko; **Page 45** (tr) Shutterstock / Fernando Duarte Nogueira, (cr) Shutterstock V/ ladislav T. Jirousek, (br) Shutterstock / Arab; **Page 46** (ca) Shutterstock / block23, (b) Shutterstock / Artush, (tr) Shutterstock / Artush; **Page 47** (t) Shutterstock / Aleksandra H. Kossowska,(b) Shutterstock / Janos Rautonen; **Page 48 (**tr) Shutterstock / Martin Mecnarowski, (tl) Shutterstock / block23, (bl) Shutterstock / Martin Mecnarowski, (br) Shutterstock / Vadim Petrakov; **Page 49** (c ) Shutterstock / Przemyslaw Skibinski, (br) Shutterstock / Angela N Perryman; **Page 50** (tr) Shutterstock / xpixel, (bl) Shutterstock / xpixel; **Page 51-52** (b) Getty Images / Premium Access E+ / cinoby; **Page 52** (tl) Alamy / fine art, (tr) Getty Images / iStock / Getty Images Plus / TadejZupancic; **Page 52-53** (b) Jeffrey Barbee; **Page 53** (tl) Getty Images / DigitalGlobe / capeWare3d / Contributor, (tr) Shutterstock / beachbassman, (cra) Shutterstock / Dylan leonard; **Page 54** (c ) Shutterstock / Makhh, (br) Shutterstock / Heidi De Koninck, (tr) Shutterstock / Damian Ryszawy; **Page 55** (tl) Shutterstock / DZiegler, (c ) Shutterstock / Kevin Benckendorf, (br) Shutterstock / Anton_Ivanov; **Page 56** (tl) Shutterstock / Makhh, (tr) Shutterstock / fanjianhua, (cr) Shutterstock / LisaSaeng, (br) Shutterstock / xuying; **Page 57** (tr) Shutterstock / gNesher, (b) Shutterstock / Hao Wan; **Page 58** (t) Shutterstock / Makhh, (bl) Alamy / National Geographic Image Collection, (br) Shutterstock / Anuradha Marwah; **Page 59** (cla) Shutterstock / Abhijeet Khedgikar, (tr) Shutterstock / Amos Chapple, (b) Alamy / Dinodia Photos; **Page 60** (t) Shutterstock / xpixel, (bl) Getty Images / iStock / Getty Images Plus / SeppFriedhuber, (tr) Shutterstock / xpixel; **Page 60-61** (b) Shutterstock / Delbars; **Page 61** (tl) Shutterstock / Marcin Szymczak, (tr) Alamy / Eyal Bartov, (cra) Shutterstock / Yury Birukov; **Page 62** (tl) Getty Images / iStock / Getty Images Plus / georgeclerk, (bl) Getty Images / iStock / Getty Images Plus / georgeclerk(tr) Getty Images / iStock / Getty Images Plus / georgeclerk, (cra) Shutterstock / Daniel Prudek; **Page 62-63** (b) Shutterstock / Vixit; **Page 63** (t) Shutterstock / Daniel Prudek, (cra) Getty Images / iStock / Getty Images Plus / abzerit; **Page 64** (ca) Shutterstock / block23, (b) Shutterstock / Nickolay Vinokurov; **Page 65** (tl) Shutterstock / Aline Fortuna, (tr) Shutterstock / Fadi Sultaneh, (b) Shutterstock / vvvita; **Page 66** (bl) Shutterstock / Roop_Dey; **Page 67** (t) Shutterstock / Travel Stock, (br) Alamy / Minden Pictures; **Page 66-67** (b) Shutterstock / Marcos del Mazo Valentin; **Page 68** (b) Shutterstock / The Wild Eyed; **Page 69** (t) Shutterstock / Deni_ Sugandi, (clb) Shutterstock / Harismoyo, (crb) Getty Images / iStock / Getty Images Plus / andersen_oystein, (br) Shutterstock / Cendrawasih Panji; **Page 70** (tl) Shutterstock / block23, (tr) Shutterstock / Heather Ruth Rose, (bl) Shutterstock / Heather Ruth Rose, (br) Shutterstock / Tom Linge; **Page 71** (tr) Shutterstock / Gaston Piccinetti, (c ) Getty Images / Moment / Julie Fletcher, (br) Shutterstock / Ioan Florin; **Page 72** (ca) Shutterstock / block23, (bl) Shutterstock / Les Scholz, (br) Shutterstock / jaytee; **Page 73** (ca) Shutterstock / Ian Woolcock, (cr) Shutterstock / Jonas J, (b) Shutterstock / Pixelheld, **Page 74-75** (tc) Shutterstock / coloursinmylife, (bc) Shutterstock / Maythee Voran; **Page 74** (ca) Shutterstock / xpixel, (bl) Shutterstock / Noradoa; **Page 75** (t) Shutterstock / AustralianCamera, (cr) Shutterstock / Luke Shelley; **Page 76** (cla) Shutterstock / block23, (br) Shutterstock / Gallinago_media; **Page 76-77** (c ) Shutterstock / Marcel Strelow; **Page 77** (t) Getty Images / iStock / Getty Images Plus / LazingBee, (cr) Shutterstock / Marcel Strelow; **Page 78** (cla) Shutterstock / block23, (tr) Getty Images / Moment / Photography by Mangiwau, (bl) Shutterstock / Barbara Ash; **Page 78-79** (b) Shutterstock / Guido Amrein Switzerland; **Page 79** (t) Getty Images / iStock / Getty Images Plus / wipusit, (clb) Getty Images / iStock / Getty Images Plus / Anzel, (crb) Shutterstock / HAFIZULLAHYATIM; **Page 80** (tr) Getty Images / iStock / Getty Images Plus / georgeclerk, (bl) Getty Images / iStock / Getty Images Plus / georgeclerk; **Page 80-81** (b) Shutterstock / Andreea Dragomir; **Page 81** (tl) Shutterstock / Arne Beruldsen, (tr) Shutterstock / Andreea Dragomir, (br) Shutterstock / vladsilver; **Page 82** (tr) Shutterstock / Dale Lorna Jacobsen, (ca) Getty Images / iStock / Getty Images Plus / georgeclerk; **Page 82-83** (b) Alamy / Cavan; **Page 83** (tl) Getty Images / iStock / Getty Images Plus / georgeclerk, (tr) Getty Images / Brand X Pictures / Science Photo Library - Seve Gschmeissner, (cr) Shutterstock / Greg-Ward; **Page 84** (cla) Shutterstock / block23, (bl) Alamy / WaterFrame; **Page 84-85** (b) Shutterstock / Alexandra Tyukavina; **Page 85** (tr) Alamy / Minden Pictures, (cra) Shutterstock / Massimiliano Finzi, (br) Alamy / Ivan Kuzmin; **Page 86** (tr)DeepSeaPhotography.com, Shutterstock / block23, (bl) Science Photo Library / Georgette Douwma, (br) Getty Images / Corbis Documentary / Ralph White; **Page 87** (c ) Getty Images / Corbis Documentary / Ralph White, (br) Getty Images / Corbis Documentary / Ralph White; **Page 88** (cla) Shutterstock / block23; **Page 89** (tl) Shutterstock / wildestanimal, (tr) Alamy / imageBROKER, (cla) Shutterstock / City Escapes Nature Photo, (cr) Alamy / Nature Picture Library; **Page 88-89** (b) Shutterstock / Dolzhenkov Pavel2; **Page 90** (tr) Alamy / Westend61 GmbH, (tl) Shutterstock / block23, (crb) Shutterstock / aquapix, (b) Alamy / Reinhard Dirscherl; **Page 91** (c ) Getty Images / Photographer's Choice / Getty Images Plus / Marco Brivio, (tr) Shutterstock / Rich Carey; **Page 92** (tl) Shutterstock / block23; **Page 92-93** (tc) Shutterstock / Andrew Astbury; **Page 92** (bl) Getty Images / iStock / Getty Images Plus / HomoCosmicos, (br) Shutterstock / Andrey Armyagov; **Page 93** (c ) Shutterstock / Andrey Armyagov.